Our Global Village

Italy

Written by: Ellen M. Dolan
Illustrated by: Ada K. Hanlon

Milliken Publishing Company   St. Louis, Missouri

For Andrea, the first *nipotina,* with love.—E.M.D.

Milliken Publishing Company
1100 Research Boulevard
St. Louis, MO 63132

Editors: Lisa Shull, Martha Kranes
Managing Editor: Kathy Hilmes

ISBN 0-7877-0041-X

A Multicultural Experience

Our Global Village hopes to share ideas, hands—on activities, and resources from other cultures which will lead you, your students, and their families in different experiences. Learning how others live, think, and react is becoming increasingly important. The earth is a global village, and each of us is quickly affected by events, styles, disasters, and ideas from far away. Old barriers of mountains and oceans are disappearing because of fax machines and airplanes. It is important to help young children learn about and value the diversity in the world around them. Fortunate is the child who has the opportunity to interact with people who speak different languages, who eat different foods, and whose skins are different colors. This child will come to appreciate the fascinating differences between people in the world while learning that people are much the same. We hope this resource series will help create a multicultural community in your classroom as you learn and share different languages, customs, and celebrations.

Metric Conversions

The purpose of this page is to aid in the conversion of measurements in this book from the English system to the metric system. Note that the tables below show two types of ounces. Liquid ounces measure the volume of a liquid and have therefore been converted into milliliters. Dry ounces, a measure of weight, have been converted into grams. Because dry substances, such as sugar and flour, may have different densities, it is advisable to measure them according to their weights in ounces rather than their volumes. The measurement unit of the cup has been reserved solely for liquid, or volume, conversions.

Conversion Formulas

when you know	formula	to find	when you know	formula	to find
teaspoons	x 5	milliliters	x .20	teaspoons	
tablespoons	x 15	milliliters	x .60	tablespoons	
fluid ounces	x 29.57	milliliters	x .03	fluid ounces	
liquid cups	x 240	milliliters	x .004	liquid cups	
US gallons	x 3.78	liters	x .26	US gallons	
dry ounces	x 28.35	grams	x .035	dry ounces	
inches	x 2.54	centimeters	x .39	inches	
square inches	x 6.45	sq. centimeters	x .15	square inches	
feet	x .30	meters	x 3.28	feet	
square feet	x .09	square meters	x 10.76	square feet	
yards	x .91	meters	x 1.09	yards	
miles	x 1.61	kilometers	x .62	miles	
square miles	x 2.59	sq. kilometers	x .40	square miles	
Fahrenheit	(°F-32)x5/9	Celsius	(°Cx9/5)+32	Fahrenheit	

Equivalent Temperatures

32°F = 0°C (water freezes)
212°F = 100°C (water boils)
350°F = 177°C
375°F = 191°C
400°F = 204°C
425°F = 218°C
450°F = 232°C

Common Cooking Conversions

1/2 cup = 120 milliliters
12 fluid ounces = 354.88 milliliters
1 quart (32 ounces) = 950 milliliters
1/2 gallon = 1.89 liters
1 Canadian gallon = 4.55 liters
8 dry ounces (1/2 pound) = 227 grams
16 dry ounces (1 pound) = 454 grams

Table of Contents

LIECHTENSTEIN

AUSTRIA

SWITZERLAND

HUNGARY

SLOVENIA

CROATIA

SERBIA

Milan

Verona

Venice

BOSNIA AND HERZ.

Turin

Ferrara

Genoa

Bologna

FRANCE

SAN MARINO

MONTENEGRO

Florence

Ligurian Sea

Pisa

Adriatic Sea

CORSICA

VATICAN Rome
CITY

SARDINIA

Naples

Tyrrhenian Sea

Ionian Sea

Mediterranean Sea

SICILY

ALGERIA

TUNISIA

Mediterranean Sea

MALTA

ITALY

Italy

Italy's geographic location in the Mediterranean Sea has brought explorers, warriors, and travelers through Italy on their way to Europe, Africa, and the Far East. These groups all helped create a rich cultural history for ancient Italy. Modern Italy was formed as a single nation only in 1861. In 1946, Italy, or "Italia" became a democratic republic.

Official Name—*Repubblica Italiana* (Italian Republic)

Area—116,320 square miles (301,268 square kilometers)

Population—58,300,000. Approximately 65% of the people live in cities and 35% live in rural areas.

Major Cities—Rome, the capital and largest city; Milan, Naples, Turin, Florence, and Venice.

Currency—1 Lira = 100 Centesini

Climate—Mild winters and hot, dry summers in central and southern Italy; cold, icy winters and frequent precipitation in mountain regions.

Elevation—Highest: Mt. Blanc 15,521 feet (4,731 meters)
Lowest: sea level

Language—The official language of Italy is Italian, a modern romance language developed from Latin.

Religion—95% of Italians are Roman Catholic. The other 5% are Protestant, Jewish, or Muslim.

Flag—The *tricolore* with three vertical stripes. Left to right, the stripes are green, white, and red.

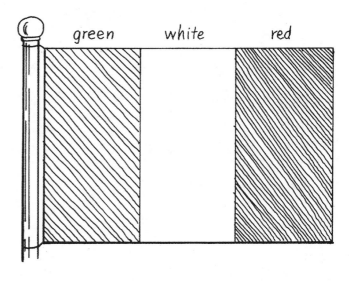

Physical Features

Italy, a peninsula in southern Europe, is easy to find on a map because of its bootlike shape. Approximately the size of Arizona, Italy juts out into the Mediterranean Sea and almost reaches the coast of North Africa. Other smaller seas making up the coast line are the Adriatic, Ionian, Tyrrhenian, and Ligurian seas. With water surrounding three sides of the land, Italy has an enormous coastline (10,000 kilometers or 6,000 miles). This helps support large shipping and fishing industries and provides miles of sandy beaches for recreation.

In addition to the peninsula, Italy's national territory includes two large islands, Sardinia and Sicily; the offshore islands of Capri, Elba, and Ischia; plus several smaller islands.

Northern Italy borders France, Switzerland, Austria, and Slovenia. The Alps, the largest mountain range in Europe, stretch across the northern border of Italy. Another mountain range, the Apennines, runs down the center of Italy. Between the Alps and the Apennines is a fertile farming area known as the Northern Plain.

The Po River flows from the Alps east to the Adriatic Sea. Other rivers include the Adige, Tiber, and Arno rivers. The largest lakes in Italy are in the Alps: Lake Garda, Lake Maggiore, and Lake Como.

The tiny Italian island of Ischia

Mount Vesuvius, an active volcano

Mount Vesuvius, near Naples and Mount Etna in Sicily are active volcanoes. In 79 A.D., Mt. Vesuvius was blown apart by a tremendous volcanic eruption which buried the ancient Roman cities, Pompeii and Herculaneum. Since then, Mt. Vesuvius has erupted 18 times; the last eruption was in 1944. Mt. Etna is 10,703 feet above sea level, the highest of Europe's active volcanoes. It last erupted in 1979. Other volcanoes in Italy include Stromboli and Vulcino.

In Your Classroom

Show the students a large map of Italy. Help them find famous cities, mountains, and islands. Then ask them to find and trace the Po River by themselves.

Point out the island of Elba where Napoleon was confined. Ask them to discover Napoleon's fate.

Have students research volcanoes and then draw a cross–section of an erupting volcano. If they are interested, tell them more about the ruins of Pompeii. They can also make a model volcano. Have students shape small pinch pots from clay. Next, they can pour a small amount of vinegar into the pot, and add a pinch of baking powder. Enjoy the eruption!

Have the students look up the word "sirocco" in the dictionary and then discover how it affects Italy. Ask them to find out where the wind comes from, how long it lasts, and why it is so hot.

As a class project, have students use clay or plaster to make a relief map of Italy; let them discover Italy's shape and interesting placement of mountain ranges. Discuss how the mountains have affected Italy as a nation.

History

Early History

Prehistory: Nomadic tribes from central Europe crossed the mountains surrounding northern Italy and began to move south and west. The tribes were mostly hunters seeking game and fish. Gradually, the hunters were replaced by agricultural settlers, who were pleased with the fertile land and the many streams and rivers of northern Italy.

Around 800 B.C.: Greeks settled the island of Sicily and planted grapes and olive groves. Etruscans began developing the area of the Po River valley and the western coast of Italy. As the Etruscans expanded their territory, many city–states, including Rome, were established.

500 B.C.–200 B.C.: Citizens of Rome began expanding throughout the peninsula and edged out the Etruscans. As Rome's strength and power grew, it came to the attention of Carthaginian General Hannibal. Hannibal planned a surprise attack on Rome. After capturing the city Saguntum in Spain, Hannibal moved up the Rhône River and into

France. With a line of elephants—the first used in battle—Hannibal and his troops crossed the Alps to invade Rome. The troops captured a few small settlements, but in the end were unsuccessful. They returned to Carthage where the Romans defeated them.

200 B.C.–400 A.D.: The Roman Empire grew and passed from one emperor to another with mixed results. The divisions between the ruling classes who lived in luxury and the masses who struggled to survive led to frequent civil wars. Under Constantine, Christians gained freedom of worship; Christianity eventually became the official religion of the Roman Empire. Later, Constantine moved the capital of the Roman Empire from Rome to Constantinople (now Istanbul, Turkey), making it the center of the Christian empire and weakening the peninsula. When Julius Caesar came to power, he decided to reorganize Italy, but was stabbed to death before he could carry out his plans. His legal heir Octavian was able to restore order. After Octavian died, several infamous leaders—Tiberius, Caligula, and Nero—controlled Rome and treated the citizens cruelly.

400 A.D.–800 A.D.: Various tribes began to invade the weakened empire. The Goths sacked Rome in 410. The Vandals attacked in 435. Romans lost many of their sources of grain and oil. Wealthy families' power and influence began to increase in city–states. Some Roman clergy also gained power and influence; they decided to make Rome the center of Christianity again, leading to two churches: the Eastern Orthodox Church in Constantinople, and the Roman Catholic Church in Rome. The religious and political power of the popes gradually increased, and by 590, Pope Gregory brought a general peace to the peninsula. In 774, Charlemagne finally drove the last tribe, the Lombards, out of Rome. When Charlemagne was crowned, Rome once more became the seat of an empire and the focus of Western religion and culture.

Renaissance

The Renaissance (rebirth) was a period of curiosity and adventure that began in Italy in the 1300s and eventually spread across Europe. It was a period in which people became interested in improving society. They looked to the ancient societies of Greece and Rome as models for their art and learning. People began to focus less on religion and more on humans and their problems.

Italy was fairly stable in the 1300s and some of its citizens had leisure time to think about art, literature, science, and philosophy. Wealthy families had a lot of power in the city–states, and they wanted to make their cities beautiful. They felt they had a duty to society. In Florence, Milan, and Venice, a handful of wealthy bankers and traders began giving money to artists, intellectuals, and others so that they could create. Architects designed and built elaborate cathedrals, plazas, fountains, and homes. New styles of

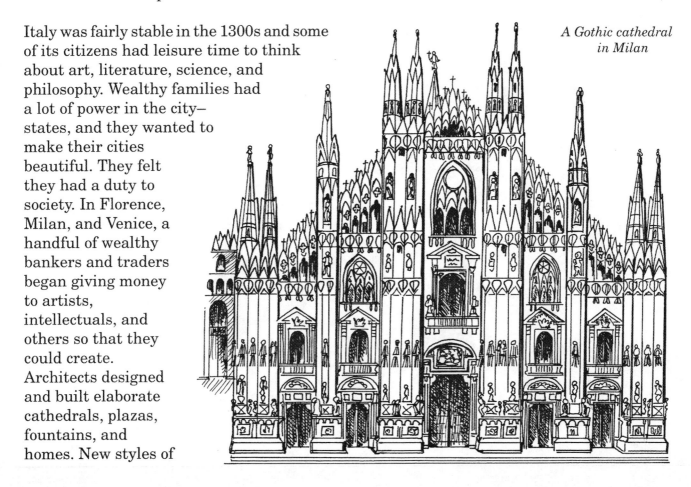

A Gothic cathedral in Milan

painting and sculpture flourished. Writers began to use the Italian language in formal writing, and musicians experimented with new ways of composing. Explorers searched for silk, spices, and other exotic products, and found new lands.

By the 1400s, merchants, bankers, diplomats, and scholars who visited Italy from Europe, had shared the new and beautiful Italian art and architecture with their countries. Renaissance ideas spread. In Italy, after this long period of peace and creativity, political stress began again. Some Italians wanted the Catholic pope as ruler, others wanted the rule of stronger city–states, and still others wanted national elections. This brought an end to the Renaissance, but Europe was now different. Italian ideals set enduring standards for art in the Western world, influenced centuries of writers and architects, and encouraged intellectual pursuits.

Modern History

Modern Italian history dates from 1870, when Italy was unified for the first time under King Victor Emmanuel II. From 1870 to 1922, Italy was governed by the king and an elected parliament. This type of government is called a "constitutional monarchy." During World War I, Italy rejected its standing alliances with Austria, Germany, and Hungary. In 1915, Italy joined the Allies and hoped to expand its territory as a reward for fighting.

The time after the war was difficult for Italians. They had expected a generous settlement of postwar land, instead of the small portion along the border of Austria which they received. Veterans and others were having difficulty finding work. While the wealthy feared the growing support for Communism among the lower classes, the majority of Italians wanted change.

Benito Mussolini

In 1922, Benito Mussolini came into power and installed a fascist dictatorship. Although the king remained head of the state, he really had little power. Mussolini wanted to rebuild the glory of the Roman Empire for Italy, and did succeed in helping the country to recover from some of the effects of the war. He put people to work again, built roads and railways, and settled old disputes between Italy and the Roman Catholic Church. On the other hand, Mussolini eliminated former political parties and opponents through murder, exile, and prison camps. He restricted many civil rights and took control of businesses, newspapers, the police, and schools.

To rebuild an empire, Italy needed to expand its territory. In 1935, Mussolini and his armies invaded and conquered Ethiopia. In 1936, they joined in Spain's civil war on the side of the dictator Francisco Franco. By 1940, and the outbreak of World War II, Mussolini had isolated Italy in the world community. The only alliance left was with Nazi Germany. But Mussolini's war efforts ran into problems on all sides. Italy was defeated in North Africa, Greece, and finally in Italy. After several defeats the king forced Mussolini to resign. Italy eventually surrendered to the Allies.

In 1946, after the war, the Italians voted to replace their monarchy—closely associated with Mussolini and fascism—with a republic. Several major and many minor political parties were formed, unlike the United States where there are only two major political parties. Italy thrived, especially in the north, for many years. In the south of Italy, the country remained poor. Many southern Italians moved north or left Italy for other countries.

Today, communism continues to gain support in Italy and the Republic has not yet solved all of the country's internal problems. However, the government has begun massive projects to improve Italian life, particularly in the south. They are working to educate and train workers, to improve roads and railways, and to better the land, in order to improve the everyday lives of the Italian citizens.

Vatican City

The Roman Catholic Church at one time owned a vast amount of property in Italy. In 1870, when Victor Emmanuel II became king, Rome was named the capital city. Church property was reduced to a 100-acre site in the center of Rome. This became known as Vatican City, home of the Roman Catholic Pope.

Vatican City has its own postal system, railroad station, newspaper, and bank. The Vatican's Swiss Guards are ceremonial escorts for the pope.

St. Peter's Church in Vatican City is one of the largest in the world. A huge *piazza*, or open square, is in front of the church. Nearby are other impressive buildings: the Vatican Palace, where the pope resides, and the Vatican Museum, which is filled with art masterpieces.

St. Peter's Church

San Marino

San Marino is a small independent republic, which is totally surrounded by Italian territory. It is about 140 miles (224 kilometers) directly north of Rome and is near the coast of the Adriatic Sea. Monte Titano, part of the Apennines mountain range, covers most of San Marino. On each of Titano's three peaks is a large medieval fortress.

Most of the people of San Marino are Roman Catholic and speak Italian. The majority work on the land, growing wheat and grapes and raising livestock. Others manufacture pottery, weave various textiles, and quarry stone. In 1862, San Marino and Italy signed a friendship treaty which has been renewed several times.

In Your Classroom

In an encyclopedia or history book, find the traditional story of the founding of Rome. Twin brothers, Romulus and Remus, were abandoned on the bank of the Tiber River. They had nearly starved when a she-wolf found them, fed them, and nursed them to health. A shepherd raised them. When the brothers were grown, they established a stronghold—Rome—on the spot where they'd been abandoned. Read the story to the students and then ask if there are any stories or myths about the founding of their city.

Ask the students to research Charlemagne, known as Charles the Great, who is considered the founder of the Holy Roman Empire. Have them write a paragraph about his life.

Have half of the students choose an Italian hero, such as Octavian, and the other half an Italian villain, such as Nero. Help them discover how each helped or hindered life for the people of Italy.

Have the students list an artistic work by the following Renaissance artist or sculptor:

Artist	Work
Fra Angelico	Annunciation
Titian	
Botticelli	
Raphael	
Donatello	
Cellini	
Michelangelo	

Other interesting Italian natives to discuss are Andrea Doria, Genoese admiral; Christopher Columbus, also born in Genoa; Enzo Ferrari, race car designer; and Sophia Loren, movie actress.

Education

Preschool programs are offered in Italy to children from 3 to 5 years old. The programs are optional and parents are charged fees. One of the schools of choice is a Montessori preschool. These were developed by Dr. Maria Montessori who taught at the University of Rome in the early 1900s. The program centers on developing a partnership between teacher and pupil. No grades are given and the teacher determines when the student is ready to move on. In addition to Montessori schools, there are many other private preschools most of which are run by religious orders.

Dr. Maria Montessori

From ages 6 to 14, children must attend school. Public schools are free, while private schools charge fees. Sometimes the children have classes on Saturdays. Children are up early to get ready for school. The girls wear casual skirts or slacks with blouses and sweaters. They enjoy choosing bright colors. The boys also dress casually. Students who do not live near their school ride a city bus across town. There are about 20 children in each class and the subjects include Italian, English, geography, math, science, history, music, technical training, physical education, and religion—even in public schools. Art classes are sometimes taught in museums if near the school. The students may all call their teacher by his or her first name. And even in Italy, the students know what "homework" is!

After primary and middle school, students may continue their studies at a classical or a scientific high school; or they may choose from a variety of technical schools which prepare them for specific careers. At the end of these five–year programs, students who wish to continue their studies must first pass an extremely difficult state exam.

Universities are crowded, so after high school, only a small percentage of students continue their studies at a university. The major universities are located in Rome, Naples, Milan, Bologna, and Turin. The University of Bologna, which was founded in the eleventh century, is the oldest university in Europe.

Language

In the fourteenth century two kinds of Latin were spoken in Italy—one by wealthy, educated people and the other by working class people. Shortly after 1300, a famous poet, Dante Alighieri, began writing a long poem, *The Divine Comedy*, in the language of the workers so that everybody could read it. Because the poem was so popular, the working people's Latin became the official language of Italy.

In grammar and vocabulary, today's Italian is much like ancient Latin. But almost every town or region in Italy has its own dialect or speech pattern.* At one time, there were as many as 1,500 dialects. These developed because the mountains in Italy kept people isolated from one another. Today, people living in Sicily may still have difficulty understanding what people in Milan say. However, mandatory education, radio, and television broadcasts have led to the widespread use of the Tuscan dialect.

Everyday Phrases in Italian

arrivederci	(ahr–REE–veh–DAYR–chee)	good–bye
bene	(BEH–nay)	well
buon giorno	(BWAWN JOHR–noh)	good day, hello
buono	(BWAW–noh)	good
come sta?	(KOH–may STAH)	how are you?
grazie	(GRAHT–see–ay)	thanks
il bambino	(eel bahm–BEE–noh)	child
il restorante	(eel REE–stoh–RAHN–tay)	the restaurant
la casa	(lah KAH–sah)	the house
per favore	(pair fah–VOH–ray)	please
scusa	(SKOO–sah)	I beg your pardon
si	(SEE)	yes
Come vi chiamate?	(KO–may vee kee–AH–mah–tay)	What is your name?
Mi chiamo _____	(Mee kee–AH–mow)	My name is _____

* In contrast, in the United States, there are regional accents and word usage. A person living in Louisiana might pronounce the word "get" differently than a person in Minnesota. In one region a utensil may be called a "pail"; in another it would be called a "bucket." Most likely, however, a person from one region could easily understand a person from another region.

In Your Classroom

Help the students to understand the meaning of "dialect."

Ask the students to write a paragraph describing recess to a classmate. Have them write a paragraph describing the same event to a parent. Ask them to discover the differences in choice of words.

Ask the students to read aloud the list of Italian words and expressions. Assign or let the students choose a partner. Have them greet and answer each other by using an Italian word or phrase.

List a few Italian proper names: Maria, Antonio, Anna, Giovanni, Gina, Mario. Ask the students to add others.

Brainstorm with your class for Italian words that are part of the English language. Many Italian words entered the English language as names for foods, especially types of pasta: lasagna, pizza, ravioli, vermicelli, fettucine, spaghetti, and so on. Other Italian words entered our language through classical music, such as the Italian word "solo" meaning alone, and words for instruments: piano, violin, cello.

Creative Arts

Italy has one of the richest traditions of art and literature in the world. In the 1300s A.D., the "Renaissance," a period of rebirth of interest in past art, began and lasted for three very productive centuries. The rivalry between the city–states of Rome, Florence, Naples, Milan, and others encouraged a high quality of artistic work during this time. The Medici, a family of wealthy bankers living in Florence during the Renaissance, encouraged and subsidized many authors and other artists, allowing them to create their art.

Architecture

One of Italy's most famous structures is the Leaning Tower of Pisa, a marble bell tower. Carved on its portal are several monsters and animals. The building of the tower began in 1174 and was finally finished in 1350—175 years later. Soon after the first three stories were built, the ground beneath the Tower began to sink. The structure tipped until it was nearly 17 feet (5 meters) out of line. The base was reinforced with concrete and has only moved about 12 inches (30.5 centimeters) in the last century. The top can be reached by climbing up the 294 stairs inside the Tower to a terrace. From this terrace, Gallileo conducted some of his famous experiments on gravity. The Tower is also considered one of the Seven Wonders of the World.

An imposing ruin is the Roman Colosseum, one of the largest buildings in the world. It was a huge stadium four stories high which held 50,000 spectators. Three stories of arcades were faced with Doric, Ionic, and Corinthian semi–columns. Dramas, gladiator challenges, and other events took place in the central arena.

The Leaning Tower of Pisa

Other famous structures in Italy include St. Peter's Church in Vatican City, the Arch of Constantine, the paved Roman road known as the Appian Way, and the Cathedral of Florence—built by the Renaissance architect Filippo Brunelleschi.

In Your Classroom

Divide the students into groups of four or five. Provide building blocks or legos and have each group build a miniature leaning tower. Set a time limit and then measure to find the highest structure. Ask the winning group to explain how they maintained balance.

Have students research the Colosseum. Ask them to compare its size to a modern stadium or arena. Help them discover what kind of sporting events took place in the arena in ancient times.

Painting and Sculpture

Italian art has been heavily influenced by the country's religion, by the likes and dislikes of its rulers, and by artists' admiration of earlier classical work of the Greeks.

Michelangelo was Italy's most talented sculptor and painter. His marble statue *Pietà* (at right) and his paintings on the ceiling of the Sistine Chapel in St. Peter's Church are his most famous works. When he was painting the ceiling, Michelangelo spent his day lying on his back in a sling, which was suspended from the top of the building. He did this for several years! In addition to being a sculptor and painter, Michelangelo was also a poet and architect.

Leonardo da Vinci, another world–famous Italian artist, lived in Florence, Italy, where the Renaissance began. He used an effective technique which softly blended colors and texture in his paintings. The *Mona Lisa* and *The Last Supper* are his most famous works. Da Vinci amazed the world with his skill in painting, but he was also an inventor, a scientist, an engineer, and an architect. He was extremely curious, and studied medicine, botany, and astronomy.

Other gifted Italian artists were Donatello and Botticelli. Luca Della Robbia developed the popular glazed terra–cotta sculptures. Modigliani, an artist in more modern times, was famous for his abstract, as well as his traditional works.

In Your Classroom

Organize a class art show. Have each student choose his or her favorite medium—chalk, paint, crayon, colored pencil—and complete a drawing. Hang the drawings around the room and have students vote on a favorite. Invite other classes to the "show."

Provide clay for each student and have them create their own sculptures. Older students could design a border or pattern (frieze) taken from a famous piece of art.

Literature

Specific Italian literature was late in developing because Latin was so widely used in formal writing. Dante Alighieri's *The Divine Comedy* was one of the first poems written in language that could be read by the common people as well as by royalty. Dante's writings helped unite the country with a common Italian language.

Other notable early writers are Francesco Petrarch, Cicero, and Giovanni Boccaccio, who wrote *The Decameron,* a collection of 100 tales about Italian life. Niccolò Machiavelli's *The Prince* has a strong political slant. Among the later well–known writers were poet Umberto Boccioni, novelist Alberto Moravia, and winners of the Nobel Prize for Literature—novelist Grazia Deledda and poet Salvatore Quasimodo. Italian writers throughout the centuries have contributed much to world literature and have greatly influenced later writers.

In Your Classroom

Have a copy of Carlo Collodi's *The Adventures of Pinocchio* available in the classroom. Read parts of it to the students. Ask them to listen for names, places, or things that suggest Italy (example: the name of the puppet maker, Guiseppi, or the villian Stromboli, named for a volcano near Sicily).

Ask the students if they know any people or organizations that support the arts today as the Medici did in Italy.

Music

In the music world, grand opera is considered to be a product of Italy. Opera, a play set to elegant music, was originally created to entertain royalty. But soon performances were opened to the public. The Italian people immediately accepted the lavish romances, comedies, and dramatic tragedies. *La Scala* or *Teatro all Scala* (Theater of the Stairs) in Milan is the most famous opera house in the world.

Guiseppe Verdi, composer of 26 operas, had a long association with La Scala. Verdi became an international figure and his work is still popular all over the world. *Rigoletto* and *La Traviata* are two of his best known operas.

Antonio Vivaldi, born in Venice, was one of Italy's leading composers and violinists. Gioacchino Rossini, a musical genius, created 40 operas. Other talented Italian musicians and composers include Niccolò Paganini, Gaetano Donizatti, Vincenzo Bellini, Giacomo Puccini, Enrico Caruso, a world–renowned tenor, and Arturo Toscanini, one of Italy's principal conductors.

Guiseppe Verde, composer of operas

In Your Classroom

Have each student choose an Italian musician and write a biographical sketch about him or her.

Let the students listen to a recording of the "William Tell Overture" (Lone Ranger theme) by Rossini. Then listen to Lucianio Pavarotti, a modern Italian tenor. (Recordings can be found in most public libraries and in university music libraries.) Encourage the students to share their reactions to the music.

The world–famous opera house, La Scala

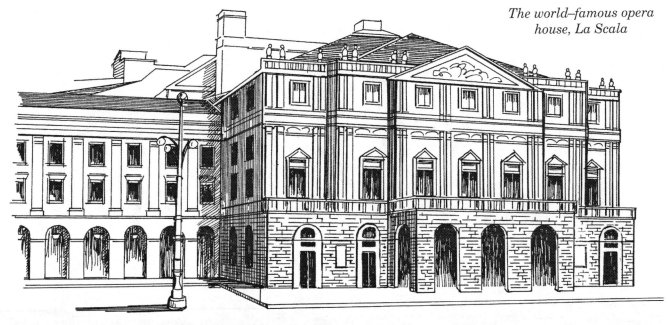

Foods

Italians enjoy their meals not only for nourishment, but also as a social part of the day. Breakfast is light and usually consists of a roll and coffee or milk. The main meal, for most Italians, is served at noon. The entire family gathers for conversation, news, and laughter, as well as for food. The meal usually begins with a pasta dish, then fish or meat, vegetables and salad, and finally fresh fruit or cheese, and coffee for dessert. Bread and wine are served throughout dinner. An evening meal could be pizza, fried potatoes, and strawberries. *Espresso,* a rich coffee, is enjoyed after the meal.

The best–known food from Italy is pasta. There are nearly 50 kinds, including fettuccini, cannelloni, ravioli, and spaghetti. "Pasta" is an Italian word meaning paste or dough. Pasta is made with hard–grained wheat, *semolina,* which is mixed with water and eggs to form a dough which is then rolled and cut into various shapes. Many Italians eat pasta every day, and sometimes twice a day. *Polenta* is a mixture of rice and cornmeal. Prosciutto ham, aged and thinly sliced, is also popular. Parmesan and mozzarella are among the many Italian cheeses.

Less than half of Italy's land is fertile. Still, the farms of the Northern Plain and southern Italy provide Italians with grapes, olives, citrus fruits, vegetables, almonds, wheat, rice, and corn. Many of these are sold at outdoor markets.

History of Pizza

The round, flat circle of dough which is the base of modern pizza has really been used for centuries. Early Romans spread bits of fish on the dough and baked it. Rural Italian women, who baked the family bread in a large community oven, flattened some of the dough and baked a disc. Gradually people began to add ingredients like tomatoes and herbs to the plain dough.

Soon bakers were opening pizza shops in small towns. One of the best bakers was Señor Esposito, who had a shop in Naples. His pizzas were filled with tomatoes and basil. One day Esposito was asked to make a special pizza for Queen Margherita.

The baker decided to include the three colors of the Italian flag—green, white, and red—to honor Margherita. On the pizza dough he spread red tomatoes, green basil, and added a new ingredient—white mozzarella cheese. This combination became popular in Italy, and later in America.

In Your Classroom

Spread a selection of dry pasta on a table or tray. Ask students to identify each kind. Let them create pictures by gluing the pasta to heavy paper and adding color with crayons or markers.

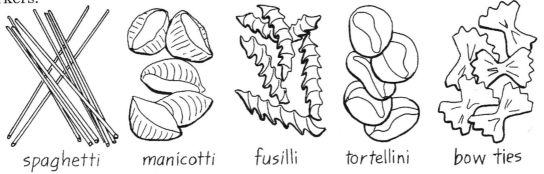

spaghetti manicotti fusilli tortellini bow ties

If a kitchen is available, prepare the following dishes with the help of the students:

Macaroni and Cheese

1 lb. macaroni
3/4 T. butter or margarine
3/4 c. Parmesan cheese
1/3 c. mozzarella cheese
1/3 c. Gruyère cheese
1 c. heavy cream
salt and pepper

Cook the macaroni in boiling, salted water until tender. Drain. Place macaroni in large bowl. Toss with the butter and cheeses. Add salt, pepper, and cream, and toss again. Bake in moderate oven (350°F) uncovered for 20 minutes or until top is browned. Serves 6 lightly.

Italian Salad

1–2 heads of shredded iceburg and romaine lettuce
1 chopped pimiento
1 jar artichoke hearts
3/4 c. olive oil
1/4 c. vinegar
1/4 c. Parmesan cheese

Combine lettuce and pimiento in a large bowl. Drain artichoke hearts, cut in half or fourths, and add to the bowl. Combine oil, vinegar, and 1/4 cup Parmesan cheese in a shaker. Mix well and pour over lettuce. Add salt, pepper, and additional parmesan cheese to taste. Serve 6 immediately.

Pizza Party

frozen 12–inch rounds of pizza dough
tomato paste
basil or other herbs
shredded cheeses
sliced vegetables, sausage slices, and other toppings desired

Allow one pizza per four students. Bake dough until partly browned. Remove from oven and cool slightly. Have students smooth paste on pizza and add herbs, cheeses, and other ingredients. Return to oven and brown carefully. Remove, slice, and enjoy.

Celebrations and Holidays

Italy is a predominantly Catholic country, so many of its holidays have a religious theme. Others mark political or national events.

Christmas
December 25

A religious holiday honoring the birth of Jesus Christ. Weeks before the holiday, the family Christmas tree is selected and decorated with ornaments and lights. Under each tree is a nativity scene with an empty cradle or manger. On Christmas day, the figure of the infant Jesus is placed in the manger. The family attends church and gathers later in the day for a festive meal. Italians say, *"Buon Natale!"*—Merry Christmas!

Epiphany
January 6

The day when the three Wise Men, bringing gifts to the Christ Child, arrived in Bethlehem. This has been the traditional day to exchange toys and gifts. Some modern families are beginning to open presents after the Christmas dinner.

Valentine's Day
February 14

Celebrates friendship, love, and courtship. On this feast day of St. Valentine, Italian children exchange friendly notes and valentines. There are also many "notes" from Cupid, the mythical son of Venus, Roman Goddess of Love.

Easter

The end of Lent and a Christian celebration of Jesus Christ's resurrection from the dead. Easter is an important religious holiday. Italian families spend much of Easter Sunday in church. On the following day, Easter Monday, families relax and frequently bring their children to a hillside or beach for a picnic.

April 21

People living in Rome mark the founding of their city in 753 B.C. by taking a holiday from work.

National Holiday
June 2

A national political holiday marking the anniversary of the founding of the Italian Republic in 1946. People celebrate with parades and meetings.

Festival of Unity

(*Festa di l'Unita*), a three week political festival held in early summer. Every night there are speakers who present different political points of view. The Festival also includes music, open–air theaters, art shows, dancing, booksellers, and food from several restaurants.

Summer Holidays

Two weeks every August. Families leave the cities to vacation in the cooler hills or at sunny beaches.

In addition to these national celebrations, there are many religious "fetes" in smaller cities that honor patron saints with processions through the streets. Children are dressed in their finest clothes and the buildings and balconies are decorated with flowers. Bands play festive music and fireworks explode at regular intervals.

In Your Classroom

Help the students to create their own school festival. Example: When was your school founded? What color decorations would you use? Would you have a parade? Would you invite parents? Would you serve special food?

Find out more about the national political holiday celebrated on June 2. Compare it to the Fourth of July (Independence Day) celebration in the United States.

Create an Italian calendar commemorating these holidays, and research other celebrations or festivals held throughout Italy. Let students discover *La Befana* and compare her to Santa Claus. Read *The Legend of Old Befana* by Tomie dePaola.

Sports and Recreation

Soccer is Italy's national sport. It is closely followed by enthusiastic fans. Nearly every city and village in the country has a team and the rivalry is intense. Young people play pick–up soccer in village squares with the hopes of one day becoming professional soccer heroes. In 1982, the Italian soccer team was the best in the world when it won the World Cup championship in Spain. In 1990, Italy hosted the World Cup matches and won third place.

Besides soccer, Italians love racing of all kinds. They have always been strong competitors in the annual Tour of Italy, a two–week bicycle race around Italy, which draws the world's top racers. Sports car racing is also very popular with both school children and adults. The Ferrari and Fiat racing cars, manufactured in Italy, are among the world's best. The Grand Prix races, a series of international races held on challenging road courses, are held each summer in Imola, Italy. Winning car drivers become instant heroes.

During regular vacations, Italian families spend time visiting Italy's southern beaches. While parents relax under huge, colorful umbrellas, children play in the sand and swim in the clear sea. Wealthier families may spend a winter vacation skiing on the slopes of the Northern Alps.

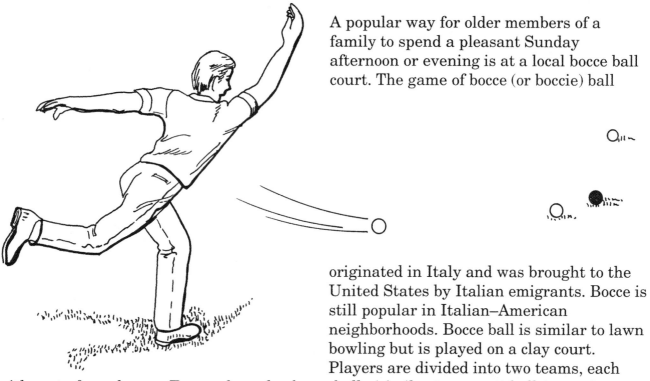

A popular way for older members of a family to spend a pleasant Sunday afternoon or evening is at a local bocce ball court. The game of bocce (or boccie) ball originated in Italy and was brought to the United States by Italian emigrants. Bocce is still popular in Italian–American neighborhoods. Bocce ball is similar to lawn bowling but is played on a clay court. Players are divided into two teams, each with up to four players. Four red wooden bocce balls (similar to croquet balls) are given to one team and four blue balls to the other. There is one smaller target ball or "palino." Play begins when one player throws or rolls the palino out onto the court. Each player's objective is to get his or her ball as close as possible to the palino. Each side has four attempts. After all balls are played, each team scores one point for each of its balls nearer the target than the opponent's. The first team to reach fifteen points is the winner.

In Your Classroom

Mark off an area approximately 20 feet by 100 feet (6 meters by 30 meters) in the classroom, gym, or playground for a bocce ball court. Croquet or tennis balls could be substituted for the regulation 5–inch (12.7–centimeter) bocce balls.

Choose two teams of four each. Remind each player that a light touch and finesse are more important than power when rolling the ball. After one game is concluded and scored, eight other students may compete. If there are enough teams in the group, a playoff round can determine the winning team.

Ask students to research Italy's sports car industry. Help them discover answers to these questions: Which car is the most popular? Where are the cars manufactured? What are their top speeds? Who are the best drivers? Where are the races held?

Have the children collect pictures of sports cars from *Car* and other magazines. Let them make trading cards by pasting the cars on thick cardboard or make a class collage on a bulletin board.

Play "Tombola," a favorite game in Italy, which is similar to Bingo. Tombola is traditionally played with friends during the Christmas period, and small gifts are given to the winners.

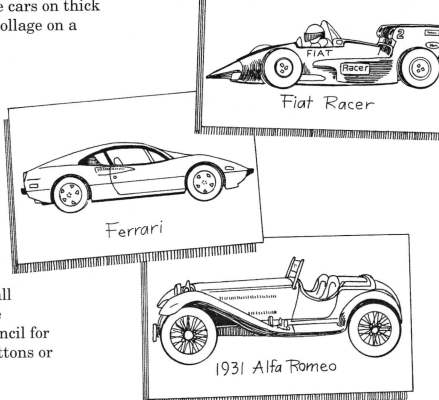

To make the game, you will need: several sheets of paper, a ruler, scissors, small paper bag or coffee can, one piece of cardboard and a pencil for every player, and lots of buttons or counters to use as covers.

1. Draw 20 small squares onto each sheet of cardboard. Write any number from 1-50 in each square.

2. Write the numbers 1-50 on a sheet of paper and cut out each number individually. Place these numbers in a paper bag or coffee can and shake.

3. Designate a caller who picks the numbers out of the bag or can, one at a time, and calls out the numbers. Players then cover the matching number on their cards. The first person to cover all of his or her numbers calls out, "Tombola," and that person is the winner.

Another game played in Italy is called Mora. It is a counting game played with fingers. Teach your children to count from one to ten in Italian. Write the numbers on the board and review them. (Use only 1-5 for younger children.) Divide the class into pairs with the players facing each other. Call out Mora, and each child simultaneously holds up any number of fingers while shouting out a guess (in Italian) as to how many fingers the other child will hold up. Whoever guesses correctly wins that round. Play to a given number of points such as five or ten.

1	uno	(OO–noh)	6	sei	(say)
2	due	(DOO–eh)	7	sette	(SEHT–teh)
3	tre	(treh)	8	otto	(OHT–toh)
4	quattro	(KWAHT–troh)	9	nove	(NOH–veh)
5	cinque	(CHEEN–kweh)	10	dieci	(DYEH–chee)

Additional Resources

Adams, Briquebec, Dramer. *Illustrated Atlas of World History.* New York: Random House, 1992.

Adleman, Robert H. and Col. George Walton. *Rome Fell Today.* Boston: Little Brown & Co, 1968.

Béthemont, Jacques, and Jean Pelletier. *Italy: A Geographical Introduction.* Longman, 1983.

Church, Alfred J. *Roman Life in the Days of Cicero.* New York: Biblo & Tannen, 1959.

Cowell, F.R. *Everyday Life in Ancient Rome.* New York: G.P. Putnam's Sons, 1961.

Crow, John A. *Italy: A Journey Through Time.* New York: Harper & Row Publishers, 1965.

Davis, John H. *Venice: Art and Life in the Lagoon City.* New York: Newsweek Book Division, 1972.

Deiss, Joseph Jay. *Herculaneum: Italy's Buried Treasure.* New York: Thomas Y. Crowell Co., 1966.

dePaola, Tomie. *Tony's Bread.* New York: Putnam Publishing Group, 1989.

———. *The Legend of Old Befana.* San Diego: Harcourt Brace Jovanovich, 1980.

———. *Merry Christmas, Strega Nona.* San Diego: Harcourt Brace Jovanovich, 1986.

———. *Strega Nona.* New York: Simon & Schuster, 1975.

DiFranco, Anthony. *Italy: Balanced on the Edge of Time.* Dillon, 1983.

Haskins, Jim. *Count Your Way Through Italy.* Minneapolis: Carolrhoda Books Inc., 1990.

Hauser, Ernest O. *Italy: A Cultural Guide.* New York: Atheneum, 1981.

Hearder, H. & D.P. Waley, eds. *A Short History of Italy.* England: Cambridge U. Press, 1963.

Johnston, Tony. *Pages of Music*. New York: Putnam Publishing Group, 1988.

Leech, Michael. *Exploring Rural Italy*. Illinois: Passport Books; National Textbook Co., 1988.

Macauly, David. *City*. Boston: Houghton Mifflin Co., 1980.

Nencini, Franco. *Florence: The Days of the Flood*. New York: Stein & Day, 1966.

Powell, Anton. *Renaissance Italy*. New York: Warwick Press, 1980.

Powers, Elizabeth. *Nero: World Leaders Past & Present*. New York: Chelsea Publishers, 1988.

Salvadori, Massimo. *Italy*. New York: Prentice–Hall, Inc., 1965.

Smart, Ted. *Italy: A Picture to Remember Her By*. Great Britain: Crescent Books, 1978.

Time–Life Books. *Italy: Library of Nations Series*. Amsterdam: TLB, Inc., 1986.

Trevelyan, Janet Penrose. *A Short History of the Italian People*. New York: Pitman Publishing Corp., 1963.

Venezia, Mike. *Da Vinci*. Chicago: Childrens Press, 1989.

Ventura, Pietro. *Venice: Birth of a City*. New York: G.P. Putnam's Sons, 1987.

Whyte, Arthur James. *Evolution of Modern Italy*. New York: W.W. Norton Co., Inc., 1965.

These offices may provide maps, additional source material, films, or souvenirs of Italy:

The local Italian Consulate or Vice–Consulate *(Check your local phone book.)*

The Italian Government Travel Office
500 North Michigan Avenue
Chicago, IL 60611
(312) 644-0990